IF YOU WERE BORN BETWEEN NOVEMBER 22 AND DECEMBER 21, THEN THIS COLORING BOOK IS MEANT FOR YOU......

MY SAGITTARIUS BIO

NAME:

DATE OF BIRTH:

TIME OF BIRTH:

PLACE OF BIRTH:

SUN SIGN: SAGITTARIUS (OR YOU GOT THE WRONG COLORING BOOK)

MOON SIGN*:

RISING SIGN*:

* FIND OUT MORE ABOUT YOUR MOON AND RISING SIGN ON SPECIALIZED ASTROLOGY WEBSITES.

©2020 Summer Belles Press.
All Rights Reserved.

☐ AGREE

☐ DISAGREE

☐ AGREE

☐ DISAGREE

☐ AGREE

☐ DISAGREE

☐ AGREE

☐ DISAGREE

☐ AGREE

☐ DISAGREE

☐ AGREE

☐ DISAGREE

☐ AGREE

☐ DISAGREE

☐ AGREE

☐ DISAGREE

☐ AGREE

☐ DISAGREE

☐ AGREE

☐ DISAGREE

☐ AGREE

☐ DISAGREE

☐ AGREE

☐ DISAGREE

☐ AGREE

☐ DISAGREE

☐ AGREE

☐ DISAGREE

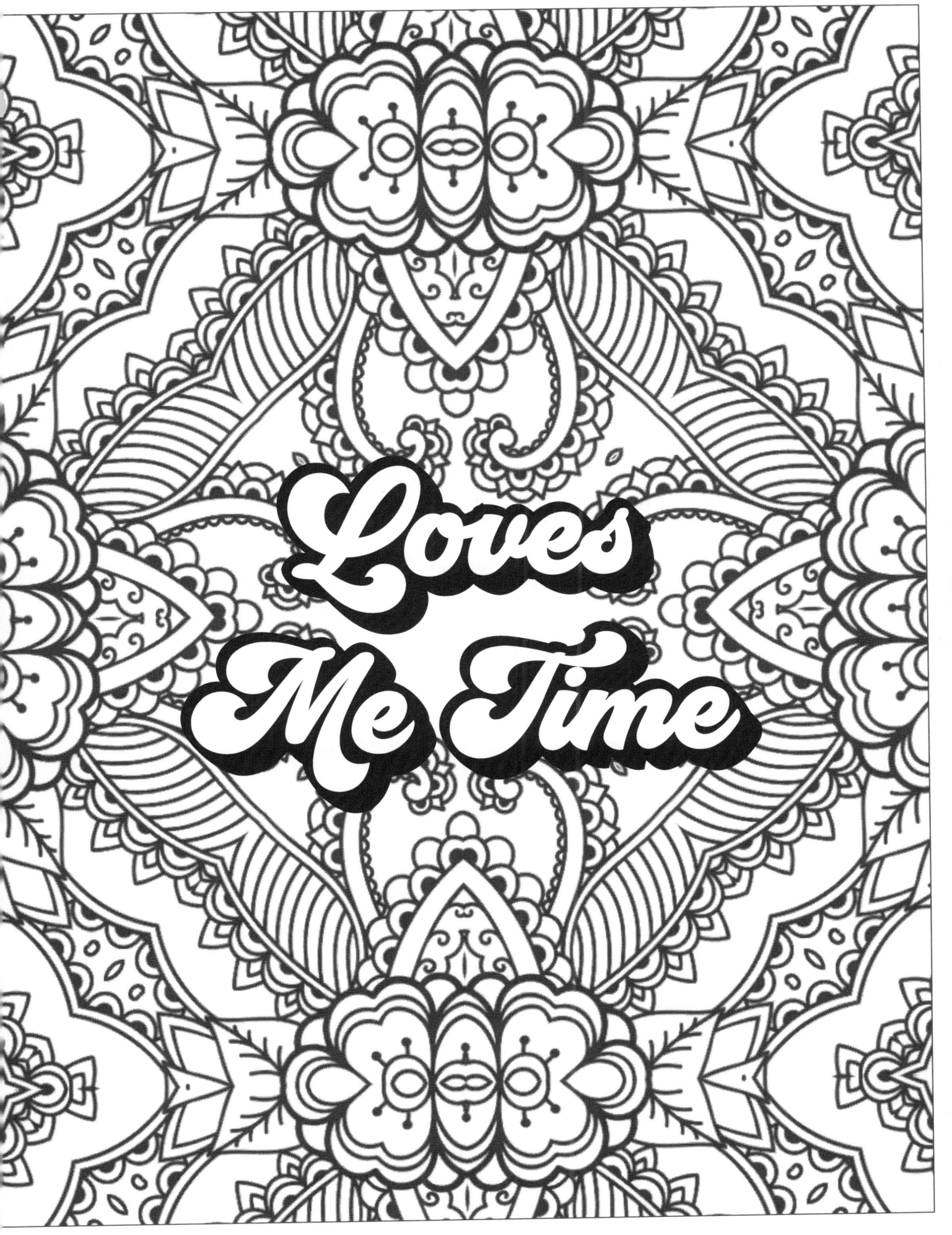

☐ AGREE

☐ DISAGREE

☐ AGREE

☐ DISAGREE

☐ AGREE

☐ DISAGREE

Never Doubt A Sagittarius

☐ AGREE

☐ DISAGREE

My Way Or The Highway

☐ AGREE

☐ DISAGREE

Destructive When Provoked

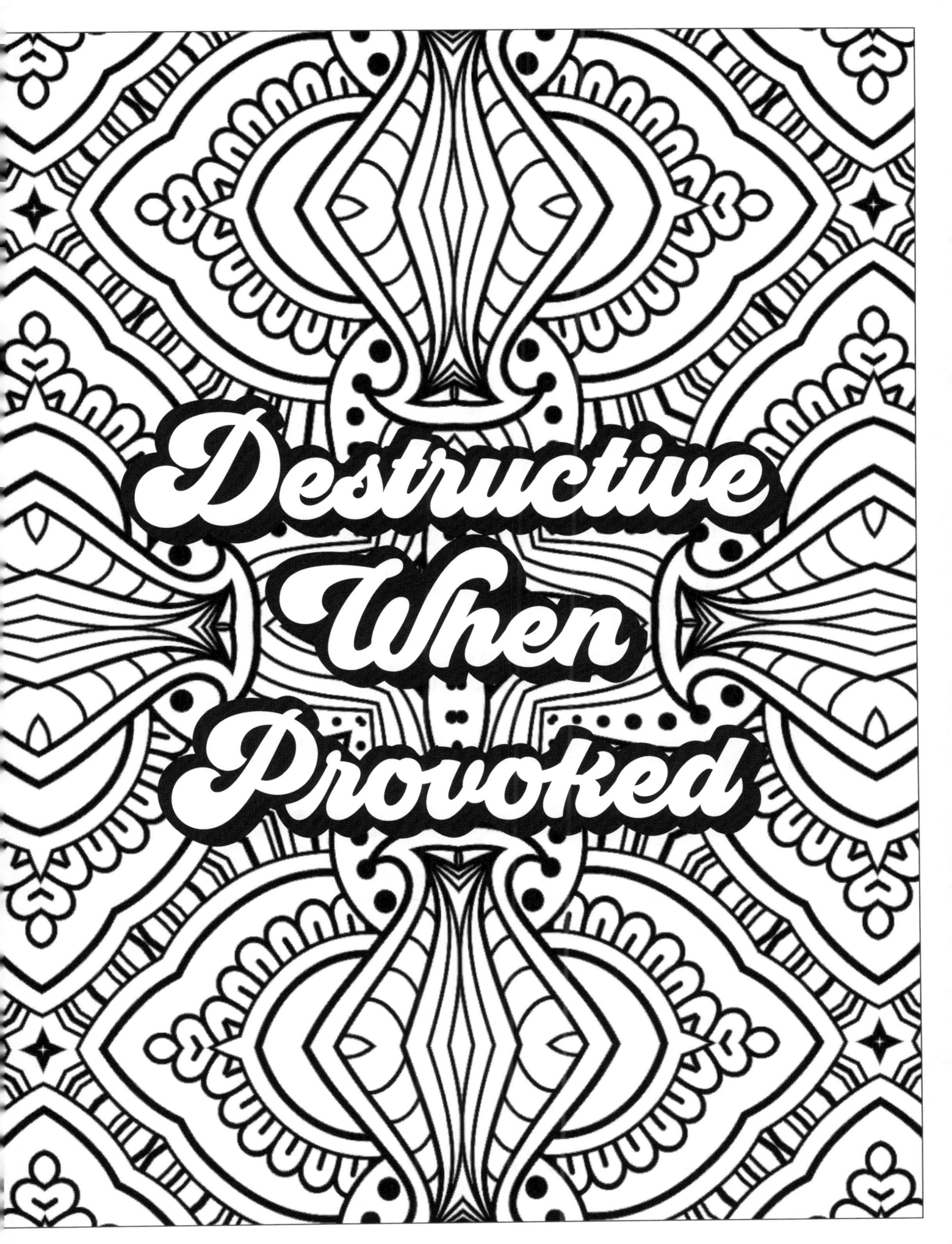

☐ AGREE

☐ DISAGREE

A Sagittarius Doesn't Need A Roadmap

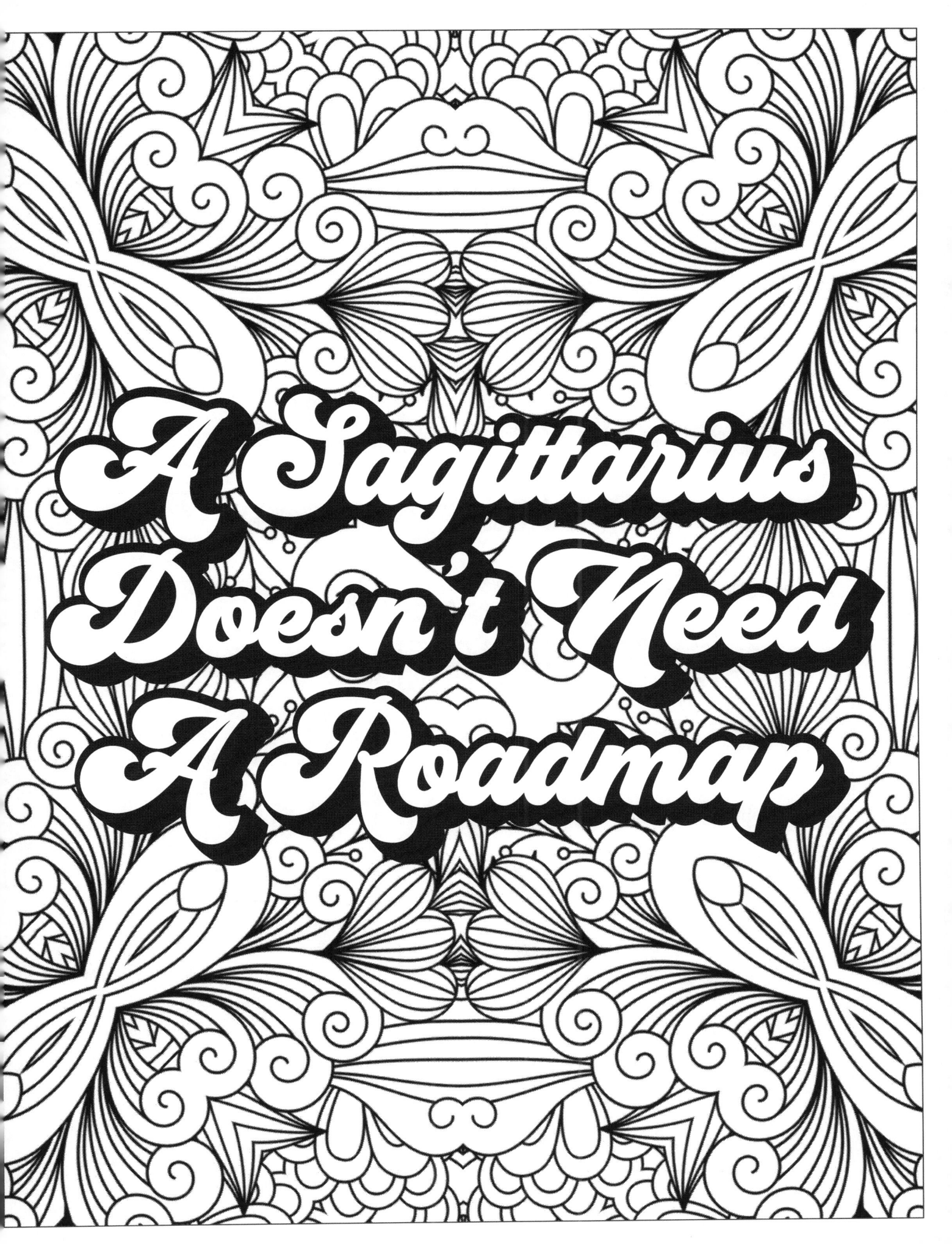

☐ AGREE

☐ DISAGREE

Loses Interest Very Fast

☐ AGREE

☐ DISAGREE

A Sagittarius Can Be Very Philosophical

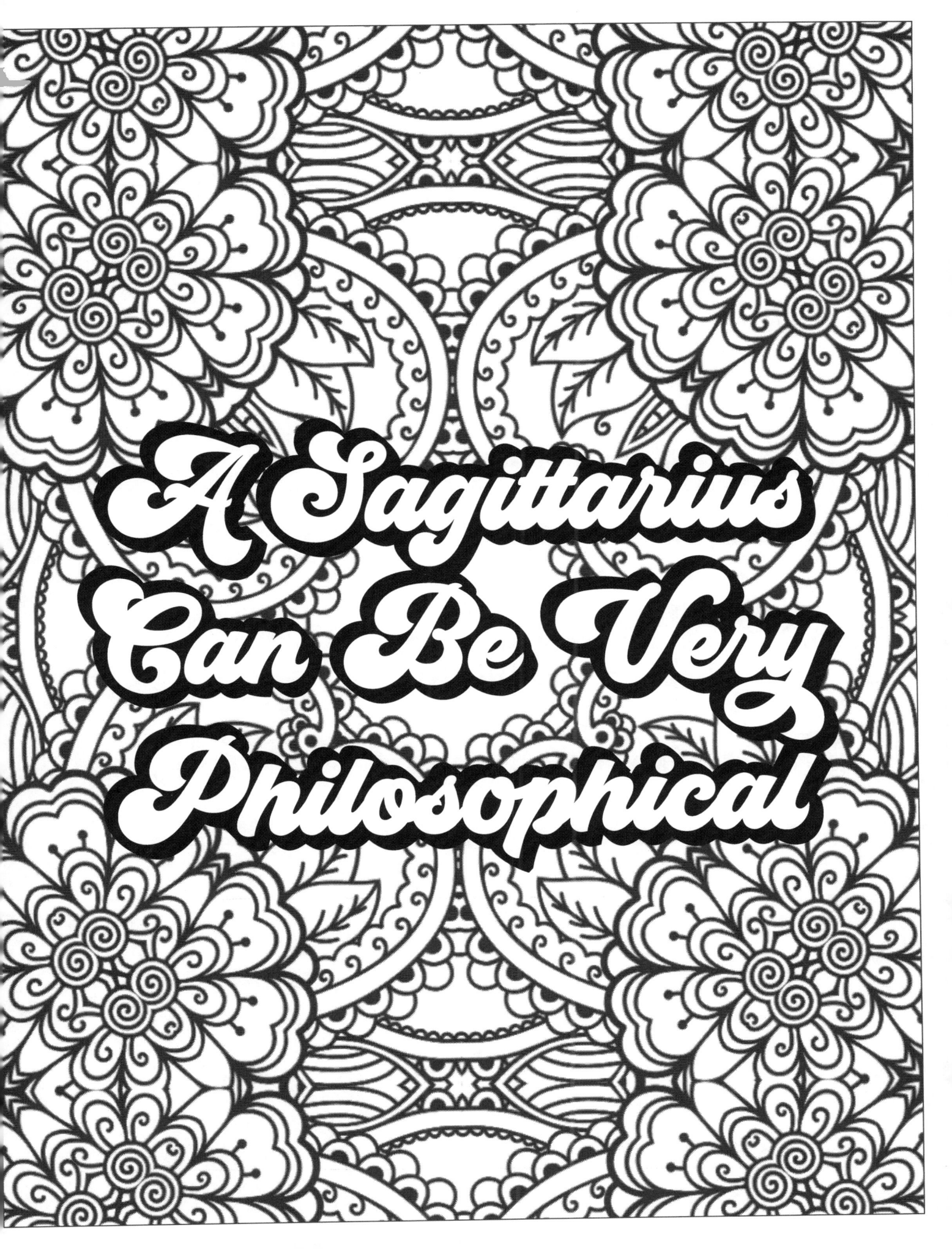

☐ AGREE

☐ DISAGREE

Born Adventurer

☐ AGREE

☐ DISAGREE

My Mind Is An Endless Labyrinth

☐ AGREE

☐ DISAGREE

Strong Sense Of Self

☐ AGREE

☐ DISAGREE

A Sagittarius Doesn't Need Other People's Approval

☐ AGREE

☐ DISAGREE

Living Life To The Fullest

☐ AGREE

☐ DISAGREE

A Sagittarius Has A Very Secret Side To Them

☐ AGREE

☐ DISAGREE

Independent & Ambitious

☐ AGREE

☐ DISAGREE

A Sagittarius Is Extremely Adaptable

Thank You!!!

Made in the USA
Columbia, SC
08 December 2023